DADDY'S HOME

YOU CAN'T SCARE HIM, HE'S A PARENT

BY ANTHONY RUBINO & GARY MARKSTEIN

First Printing: 2014

ISBN 9781483419480

U.S. trade bookstores and wholesalers and press: please contact: *Rubinocreative@aol.com*
www.daddyshomepage.com
Daddy's Home comics is distributed, worldwide by Creators Syndicate

PELECANUS PRESS

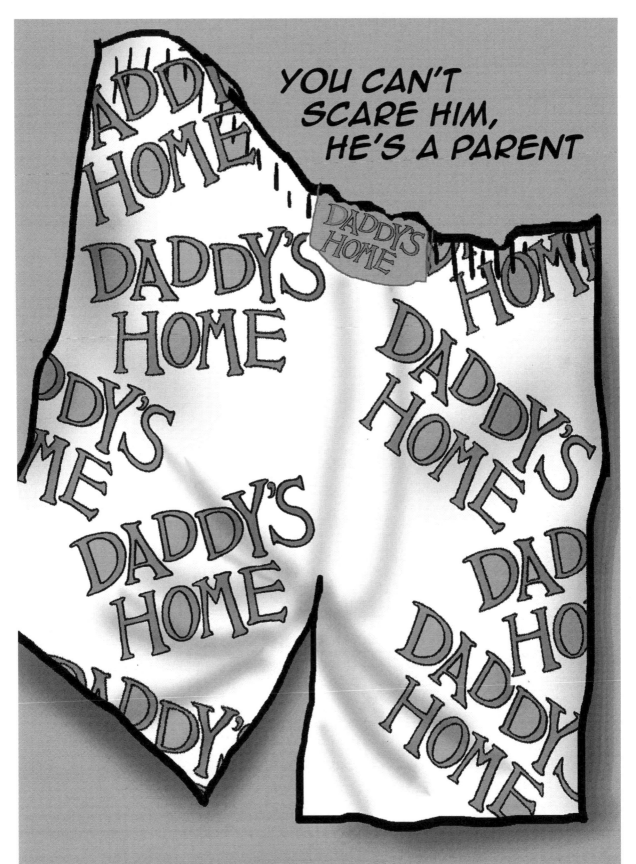

For my Father.

— *TONY*

————————————

For my sons, Blake and Grant.

— *GARY*

————————————

Thanks to our editor, Jessica Burch,
our colorist, Pete Kaminski, Creator's Syndicate
and all our client newspapers, publications and websites.

Special thanks to you, our readers.

And, to Orrin Brewster... wherever you are.

Foreword
By Professor Ellyn Lem, University of Wisconsin-Waukesha

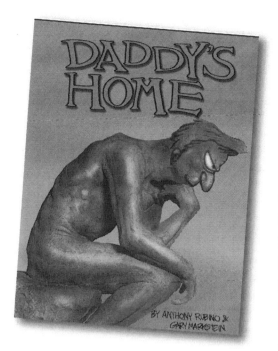

There is little agreement among the members of my family. On a given morning, my husband will eat granola; one child will eat toaster waffles — the other one might grab a bagel; I skip it altogether. Amid all this disunity, especially around food, there is something that my whole family appreciates, something that we look forward to, chuckle over together, and often discuss. What is that commonality? *Daddy's Home*. How is it that a single cartoon could capture the hearts of a college professor, a therapist, a freshman in high school and a fifth grader? The realistic depiction of family life certainly helps. Even if the family dynamics of stay-at-home dad, Pete don't match our own exactly, the humor is relatable as the son Elliot's antics mirror the hijinks of many youth today — from his constantly forgetting his backpack for school or giving his teacher a creative excuse for missing homework: "my cloud ate it!"

Daddy's Home also includes witty banter from some of its supporting characters. Pete and his neighbor Stan often exchange playful insults like the time Stan asks Pete if he accepted his friend request. Pete responds by saying that if he wanted to be rejected, he would hug his son in public. The cartoon also provides amusing reflections on contemporary happenings from the Olympics, various holidays and the weather, but can also have serious moments like the comic that featured Nelson Mandela and Martin Luther King, Jr., meeting up in heaven.

As a researcher on gender issues, I have taken a particular interest in *Daddy's Home* for its honest depiction of a household breaking traditional gender roles. We see Pete's working wife, Peggy, delight in her husband's taking on household tasks like vacuuming and hanging up newly dry-cleaned curtains, subtly sending the message to other men about the degree to which women appreciate men who share in domestic chores. Research shows that even working mothers generally do about 2/3 of work around the house, and the comic strip subtly recognizes women's efforts both at work and at home. One of my favorites that makes this point has Pete worried about how he is going to make dinner and do the laundry and meet his deadline since he works at home as a copywriter. Elliot reassures him that he will not have to do everything by himself; when Pete seems relieved, assuming Elliot will help him, his son instead adds, "It's about time mom started pulling her weight around here." That comic shows support for women in that Pete's dilemma is one that many women who are trying to balance work and family life face every day, and we recognize in Elliot's response the irony of his saying Peggy should be doing more.

It is because Daddy's Home offers social commentary on changes within the American family that I have included analysis of the comic in my forthcoming book *Can Anyone Have it All: Popular Culture's Representations of the Work-Family Conundrum* (Mellen Press) and in conference talks and public lectures that I have given. Stay-at-home fathers are still a fairly rare entity in the United States. Due to the infrequency of such an arrangement, society still tends to question this choice and look askance at men who opt to take this path, even though it opens up options for working mothers and allows dads hands-on fathering time. In my book, I demonstrate how *Daddy's Home* shows the negative feedback these fathers might face in Stan's needling of Pete with comments like "What do you do at home all day while the little lady works... crochet?" Rather than leave these insults unchecked, the comic offers clever retorts that bolster support for these dads who are taking on this role that has many benefits, ultimately, validating this choice for men. The comic strip is ripe for analysis because it does not oversimplify stay-at-home fathers as just fodder for laughs. One strip shows impoverished men in 1929 standing in line for a soup kitchen with apparently unemployed men in 2009 standing in line to pick their kids up at the bus. The message communicated is that for some men, becoming a stay-at-home father derived out of economic factors. Another *Daddy's Home* comic that I include in my book has Pete cleaning the oven when Peggy walks in from work and asks "how's it goin'?" His response, "Oh, you know, livin' the dream" can be taken multiple ways — sarcastically, since he is doing an unpleasant task or actually positive in the larger sense since he has freedom from the confines of office life and the pride of taking care of family needs. The beauty of the comic is that both interpretations could be right.

Even though we see Elliot still looking to his mom for assistance with homework or making something for a bake sale — ultimately, *Daddy's Home* shows us a competent father who can cook (sort of), and take on a number of other important roles in the family home competently, and, amusingly, which is revolutionary in comics and in popular culture in general. *Daddy's Home*, then, is breaking new and important ground, while still remembering to make us smile and making families like mine realize maybe we are not that different from one another after all.

Professor Ellyn Lem
Associate Professor of English, Honors Program Coordinator and Advisor to the UW-Waukesha Student Veterans, University of Wisconsin-Waukesha

Preface

Have you ever had one of those magical, perfect days when everything is just going your way?

Yeah, me neither.

Most of us don't. And if you do have those days then you're either delusional or drunk. Either way, good for you!

For the rest of us there's *Daddy's Home*, where our star, Pete, navigates the raw, turbulent waters of a *real-life* modern family. He does this with humor, grace and a hint of sarcasm. Okay, *mostly* sarcasm. Humor? Sure. Grace? *Meh.*

Daddy's Home is a family comic with an emphasis on the role of the modern father. Through the eyes of Pete, a working, stay-at-home dad, *DH* gives us permission to laugh at the ins-and-outs of the day-to-day.

Sure, it looks at domesticity from a male perspective, but it remains appealing to the whole family. Women like it because it makes fun of men. Kids dig it because it lampoons parents. And men, well, they just "get it."

Launched in 2008 and distributed worldwide, *Daddy's Home* has enjoyed success in some of the biggest newspapers in the US and Canada and on countless websites allowing it a circulation in the tens of millions.

This first collection, features a carefully curated batch of *your* favorites, with "behind the scenes," comments throughout.

If you like reading these comics half as much as we love making them for you, then we've done our jobs.

Now, turn the page and — for a little while, at least — don't sweat the small stuff... Just go ahead and *laugh at it.*

The Cast

 **Pete** (the husband and dad) is a stay-at-home, freelance copywriter and would-be novelist (pretty much in that order). He works hard and rests even harder.

 **Elliot** (the son) is a smart kid with a smart mouth. Pete's sometime-partner-in-crime, he's close to his Dad and relies on him for more than he's prepared to admit. He's also an independent kid — a tendency his parents encourage when it's not life threatening.

 **Peg** (the wife and mom) is a smart, educated woman with a full-time job. She likes things to be organized a certain way. And by "a certain way" she means, "her way." She's a loving and nurturing mother and is, really, a "big softy" on the inside. But don't tell her I said so.

 **Maria** (the friend) is Elliot's pal. She's mischievous, sarcastic, and lots of fun — everything you'd want in a best buddy, and accomplice. Although they're about the same age, she's a bit more mature than Elliot. Or, does she just think she is? Depends who you ask.

 **Stan** (the not-so-wacky neighbor) is consistently critical of... well, of everything. If you don't like his opinion, just wait a minute. He's got plenty of others.

 **Spork** (the early-20-something) is Peg's nephew. He's staying with the family while on the prowl for love and a job — in that order — with the job coming in a distant second. Spork is a new addition to *DH* and so is not featured all that often in this collection. But you'll get the gist.

A note about the comics featured in this collection:
We tried our best to span the entire breadth of Daddy's Home's seven years and counting. But that includes more than 2500 strips. So the bulk, but not all, of the comics here originally ran from 2009 to 2013 (though there are many more recent strips peppered throughout). Not to worry. Our next book will catch you up on the best of the rest. Also, please note that the contents of the printed version are in black and white, while the eBook is in full color.

BY "STREAK-FREE" Anthony Rubino, jr.
and "LEMONY-FRESH" Gary Markstein

WARNING

Recommended usage: *Read product twice daily for relief of minor pain and itching.*
This product may cause minor pain and itching twice daily. If itching persists, go ahead and scratch. If minor pain persists just think about how itchy you are. If depression, listlessness and general feelings of dissatisfaction occur, hey join the club. Do not leave the room after reading this product, because people remaining in the room will wait until you're gone and then talk about you. Do not read "cute" comics while reading this product as it tends to cause cartoon themes based on adorable little dogs and cats to enrage. Avoid walking into the light after reading this product. You may be dying... which has nothing to do with this product. I'm just sayin'. This product has been tested on small, defenseless, furry mammals with big, huge, dewy eyes. Mostly rats, though. We had to teach them to read first which was a whole thing. We'd like to take this opportunity to give a shout out to all the laboratory rats who are reading this now. *Way to go!* Still, no animals were harmed during the making of this product. Except for that one hamster... but he had it coming. He was a real wiseguy. Thought he was *soooo* smart. Stupid hamster. This product is non-addicting. Your insatiable need to read more and more of it is because you are weak. Do not attempt to borrow money from friends and family while reading this product. Not because of the product, it's just a bad idea.

DADDY'S HOME

BY ANTHONY RUBINO & GARY MARKSTEIN

NOTE: *The cartoons on these right-side pages (odd numbers) feature, mostly, Sunday cartoons. The cartoons on left-side pages (even numbers) are daily (weekday) comics.*

In addition to it's distribution in the US, Daddy's Home has a pretty big following in Canada. Remember when France thought Jerry Lewis was a genius? Well, that's us in Canada. With the funny woids and the pictures and the joking! Hey Laaady!

TONY RUBINO & GARY MARKSTEIN — 15

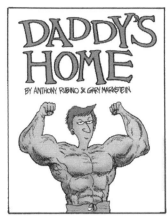

Weekday strips are colorized at our distributor, Creators Syndicate. Gary does both the inking and color for the Sundays (above). Our colorist, Pete Kaminski, is terrific, but you can really see the difference when Gary has control of the whole process*

*That is, if you're reading the EBook version. The print version is in black and white, but even there you can tell the difference in the richness of the tones.

When you render a comic strip you have to convey a lot in a very small space. I purposely gave all the characters in Daddy's Home first names with as few letters as possible so we'd have more room in the dialog balloons for the jokes, which I write as concisely as possible. This, ultimately, leaves more space for the art*.

*That's not a joke.

TONY RUBINO & GARY MARKSTEIN — 19

Visit The Daddy's Home Store: http://www.cafepress.com/daddyshomestore

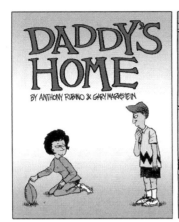

"Where do you get your ideas?" We get that question a lot. Personal experience plays a big part. I wrote the story arc (opposite page) after attending a wedding. A good amount of it actually happened.

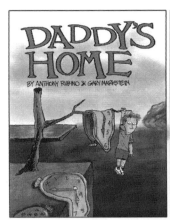

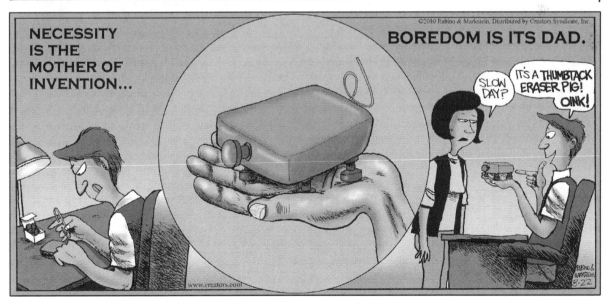

Pete's laptop used to be sentient (page 58, bottom). I stopped writing it that way, so as not to enrage our computer overlords after the machines enslave mankind and take over the planet. Why end up working in the silicon mines if you can avoid it, am I right?

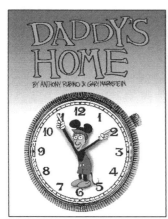

Yes, that's a bird — a pelican (bottom). He stayed with the family for a time in 2010. More on him later.

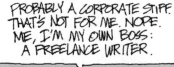

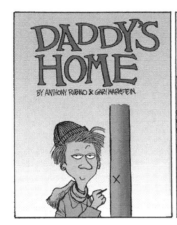

happy father's day

The last name of the family in Daddy's Home has never been revealed. It's just one of those mysterious things we may never know — like why that iceberg made the Titanic burst into flames and disappear in the Bermuda Triangle*. *Of course, I'm kidding. Everybody knows that was the Hindenburg. What? Too soon?

The original art for the comic is BIG! It's rendered about 10 times larger than it appears in print.

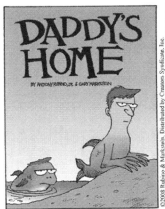

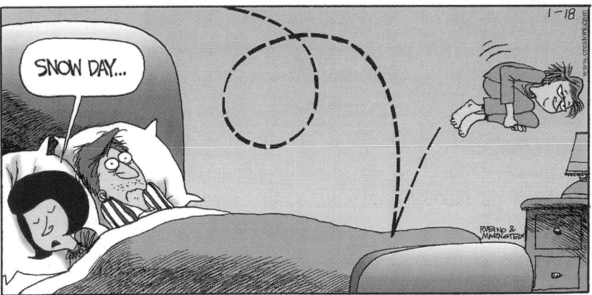

Gary's editorial cartoons have appeared hundreds of publications including; Time,
U.S. News and World Report and Newsweek. He's even had a cartoon on the cover of Newsweek. See them
here: http://www.gocomics.com/garymarkstein

With very few exceptions, I write Daddy's Home and Gary illustrates it.

Check out DADDY'S HOME at: "Peter's Daddy's Home" on Facebook and at twitter.com/daddyshomepete

Since 2008 we've published a new comic, 7 days-a-week, 365 days a year, without exception (holidays included). I'm not complaining. I'm just sayin.'

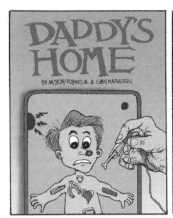

Daddy's Home isn't "political." But since Gary has the chops to do caricature I occasionally lean in that direction and write in someone you might recognize (bottom). Why not, right?

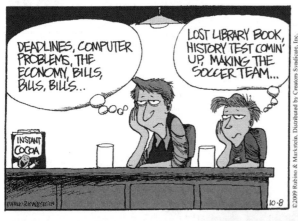

We'll often depart from the strip's normal setting completely. Usually during holidays. Some cartoonists consider this taboo, but we're not two of those cartoonists. In my opinion, one of the advantages of this medium is in its potential breadth and multiplicity. That's Pete as Columbus (bottom). The alien is a temp.

Gary and I never take a day off, but every summer the family goes on vacation for a week.
It's in their contracts. #%!@ actors! Whataya gonna do?

IT'S, LIKE, 150 MEGABYTES, SO YOU CAN BURN IT TO A CD OR JUST USE A FLASH DRIVE.

2-23

WHAT?

I LOVE IT WHEN YOU TALK NERDY TO ME.

I CAN'T BELIEVE YOU WON'T LET ME GO!

I FEEL TERRIBLE, PETER.

HE'LL UNDERSTAND WHEN HE GETS OLDER.

I GUESS THAT MAKES ME FEEL A LITTLE BETTER.

'COURSE, BY THEN IT'LL BE TOO LATE.

YOU JUST DON'T KNOW WHEN TO QUIT, DO YOU?

HOW WAS YOUR DAY?

SCHOOL...PEER PRESSURE... TEACHERS IN HUSH PUPPIES... BLAH, BLAH...

10-14

YOURS?

WORK...UNDERPAID FREELANCE WRITING...WISEGUY FOR A SON... YADDA, YADDA...

10-15

DAD, DO BABIES REALLY GET MADE THE WAY EDDIE FINKLE SAYS? AND DID YOU AND MOM DO THAT TO HAVE ME?

UHH...

WHAT ARE YOU DOING?

PLANNING MY ESCAPE ROUTE.

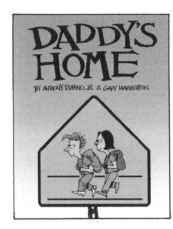

Gary's comics first appeared in print in the student newspaper at Arizona State University, where he majored in graphic design.

Weekday or, "Daily" Daddy's Home comics are completed approximately 4 weeks in advance of publication. Sunday comics are done 6 weeks in advance. We get fined by our syndicate if we're late. For real!

TONY RUBINO & GARY MARKSTEIN — 53

The nameless pelican (top) was adopted by the family in 2010 after they rescued him from the oil spill in the Gulf of Mexico. The family spent their summer vacation helping with the clean-up. We produced a pretty effective, week-long series to raise funds for — and awareness of — the spill.

The first comic strip Gary and I proposed to Creators Syndicate was completely different. The original concept featured Stan (bottom) as the main character in a strip about a inter-racial married couple. We changed the theme to Daddy's Home when Creators informed us that they were already working on a similar comic.

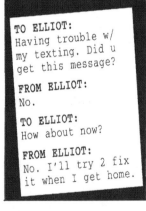

Pete's notorious for being a bit tardy in taking down his Christmas decorations (bottom).
This Sunday strip ran on March 27th.

TRANSLATION:
Why, that scamp Elliot has once again inadvertently left a Lego on the floor. And now I've happened upon it with my bare foot. Ah, well... such is life.

Me: I also dabble in fine art among other things. Check it out: http://tony-rubino.artistwebsites.com

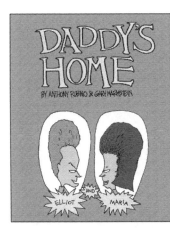

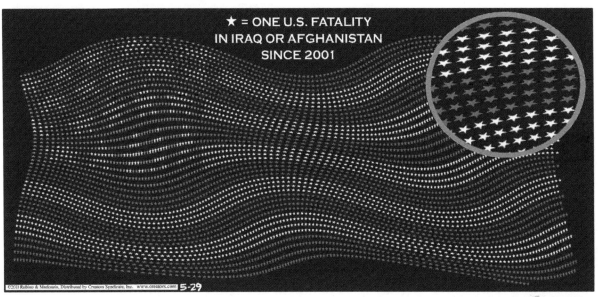

Sarcastic and self-deprecating as Daddy's Home can be, it's also proudly patriotic (center) and sentimental (bottom), from time to time. As you'll see, our, rare, serious side shines through — usually around Memorial Day, Veterans Day and in times of national and world adversity.

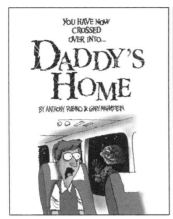

Tony's writing and cartoons have appeared in MAD Magazine, Cracked, National Lampoon, Popular Electronics and Sassy. Yes, Sassy! Also on tee shirts, greeting cards and posters sold in stores like Bloomingdales, Wal-Mart, Barnes and Noble, Spencers, and Cracker Barrel. Yes, Cracker Barrel! He also tends to randomly write about himself in the third person like some kinda bigshot.

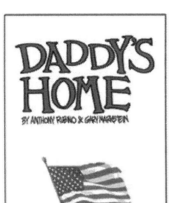

One World Trade Center construction is underway. It will be the tallest building in the United States, and among the tallest buildings in the world.

On the 10th anniversary of 9/11 we were fortunate enough to be one of more than 90 comics, with five different syndicates, who banded together to dedicate our strips in remembrance (center). I was invited to participate in a symposium about it at the New York Society of Illustrators and we were featured in several articles. Among them this piece by the Associated Press, appearing here in the Huffington Post: http://huff.to/1kriQs8

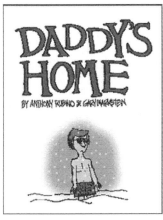

A turning point for Gary was when he drew one of his first caricatures, Richard Nixon, in a fifth-grade drafting class. His classmates went crazy over it, and he was hooked.

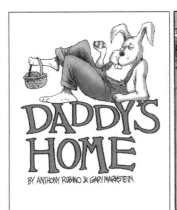

Every DH Sunday comic contains a "throw-away" panel: a portion of a Sunday comic that complements the main part of that day's comic, but is not needed for the comic to make sense. It's there to be used if newspapers and websites have space and discarded if not. You can see how this works if you compare the comic at the top of this page (with throw-away panel), with the 2 comics under it (sans throw-away).

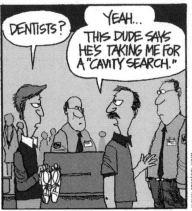

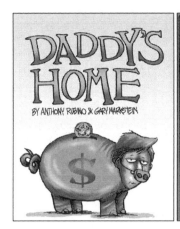

Become one of Daddy's Home's followers on Twitter: https://twitter.com/daddyshomepete
There are tens of thousands of followers... they can't ALL be drunk, right?

The family dynamic in DH is complex. Sure, they can be a sarcastic bunch and they fight but they love and care for one another through it all, as seen in this story arc (left page and page 78), where Pete and Elliot attempt — albeit badly — to care for an under-the-weather Peg. It's a challenge to write, but I do my best to show the love while they remain true to their characters.

The first time I had a comic appear in print was when I was a student at The American University, in Washington, DC, where I did a weekly comic for the school newspaper, The Eagle. The first time I was paid for a cartoon was a few months after I graduated. It appeared in Popular Electronics Magazine. It showed a kid in a doctor's office with a monitor for a head. The doctor says to the mom, "Your son has a computer virus." Yeah, I know. But, back then that was hilarious!

Gary's amazing illustration versatility really shines when I write something "outside the box." A great example is the Christmas Eve/Batman parody (above, center). And one of many good examples of us sticking to our mission to give the male perspective can be seen on the previous page (second from top).

We tried something new and rendered this 4th of July cartoon sideways. Ya know, just for grins (bottom... obviously).

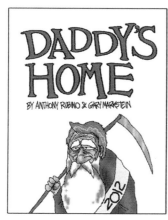  

In addition to being a syndicated editorial cartoonist, Gary was the Staff Editorial Cartoonist for *The Milwaukee Journal Sentinel*. An incredible rarity these days, as most papers can no longer afford to employ staff cartoonists. In this sense, Gary was one of the last of a dying breed.

F STANDS FOR THE CURSING THAT HE ALTERS

A IS FOR HIS ANSWERS TO MY QUESTIONS

T IS FOR THE TROUBLE WE GET IN TOGETHER

H IS FOR HIS INTERESTING SENSE OF HUMOR

DH Production Breakdown: *I write the dialog and scene descriptions as "raw scripts" then email them to Gary. Gary interprets them, inks them in black and white and sends them back to me. Once finalized they are sent to our editor at Creators Syndicate. After editing they're sent to a colorist (only the dailies. Gary does color on Sunday strips). They are then distributed to our client publications by Creators Syndicate.*

Daddy's Home Caption Contests: *Every now and then we let the lunatics run the asylum and hold a caption contest. We publish a toon sans caption (center) and let you guys test your cartooning mettle. Then we list the best entries and ask readers to vote for their favorite. The winner gets credit for the gag (bottom), a signed print of the comic and if we're feeling really generous a DH tee shirt. We really have no idea what the caption should be in these when I write the setup and Gary draws them.*

FROM THE "DADDY DICTIONARY"

Chirpacabra

1. A mysterious, allusive, intermittent, chirping noise — likely a low battery alert from one of several *smoke, gas, particle, fire, radon, security* or *carbon monoxide detectors* in your home.

SHH! SHH! SHH! SHH! THERE IT IS AGAIN!

"CHIRP"

5-16

RUBINO & MARKSTEIN

SAYS HERE YOU CAN NOW BUY AN ATTACHABLE GRANITE TABLET THAT ADDS DIGITAL DATA TO YOUR CEMETERY HEADSTONE.

I'M STILL WAITIN' FOR MY JETPACK AND **THAT'S** WHAT THEY'RE WORKING ON?!

7-22

...DRIFTED OFF THERE FOR A MINUTE. WHAT WERE YOU SAYING?

I'M SORRY. DID YOU SAY SOMETHING?

DADDY'S HOME PHILOSOPHY 101

IF A HUSBAND AND WIFE ARE TALKING IN THE WOODS, BUT NEITHER ONE IS LISTENING...

DO THEY MAKE A SOUND?

7-24

www.creators.com ©2010 Rubino & Markstein, Distributed by Creators Syndicate, Inc.

ARGUING WITH YOU ISN'T FAIR BECAUSE YOU HAVE TOTAL RECALL AND WE DON'T!

SINCE YOU REMEMBER NOTHING, HOW DO YOU KNOW I'M NOT JUST MAKING STUFF UP?

YEAH

KEEPS 'EM ON THEIR TOES, LADIES.

WINK

From time to time readers will ask me why Pete bothers talking to Stan at all (center and bottom), since he's so negative most of the time. At first I wasn't sure. But I gradually realized that Pete is attracted to Stan's cynicism because Pete isn't entirely sure he is not, himself, a cynic. He uses Stan to try and work out whether his glass is "half empty" or "half full." The jury is still out on that verdict and probably always will be for Pete.

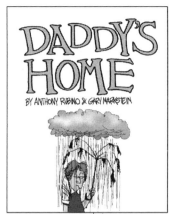

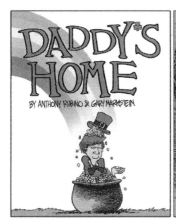

Par for course, we do our best to provide accurate and entertaining "guys' perspective stuff" concerning married life because, well... it's about a guy, right? Some good examples (left page, top and above, center).

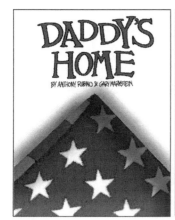

A powerful Memorial Day image (top) and an example of not taking ourselves very seriously while breaking "the fourth wall" — which we often do (bottom), shows two sides of Daddy's Home.

MEN BEHAVING BALDLY

Gary inks all the illustrations and lettering in DH by hand. We use computers only for colorization.

After Hurricane Sandy hit the East Coast, Daddy's Home teamed up with, The American Red Cross, The Salvation Army, AmeriCares, Feeding America and other relief organizations and tried to do our part to help. We did a week-long story arc revolving around Sandy relief and restoration efforts (previous page and above). Inspired readers were given the opportunity to take action, with the strip featuring a "How You Can Help" box directing readers to relief organization websites. We did a similar campaign in 2010 after the oil spill in the Gulf of Mexico (that's where the family found the pelican).

Cartoon syndication is brutally competitive. For example, Daddy's Home was one of around 6,000 submissions the five, major cartoon syndicates might receive per year, out of which two will be accepted and one actually launched. That's about a 0.016% chance of syndication. Statistically, a person has a 10-times better chance of becoming a player in the NFL. 'Course the NFL pays better. That said, cartoonists have much lower chances of receiving catastrophic knee injuries. So we got that goin' for us... which is nice.

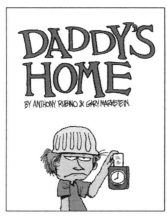

OK, yeah, I have some "bad underwear" (left page, third from top). Oh what?! Like you don't!?

Cartoon artists are held up to some very restrictive censorship standards. We can't say things and cover topics that other mediums are free to exploit. It's a bit silly as I think our readers can certainly "handle it," but that's what the newspaper editors demand. My frustration sometimes takes the form of lampooning this practice (bottom).

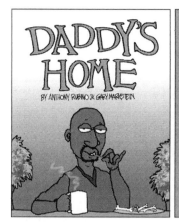

T. TURKEY
DEVOTED HUSBAND
LOVING FATHER
DELICIOUS ENTREE

IT'S SO... HI-DEF!

HAPPY HALLOWEEN FROM DADDY'S HOME

Daddy's Home is one of less than 400 active comic strips, in the world, currently available for mainstream distribution by 5 major cartoon syndicates.

My first syndication gig was with Tribune Media where I wrote and illustrated a weekly feature for their College Press Service. There I produced a comic called Wild Kingdom, which was a spin-off of the toon I did for my college newspaper at The American University. It was the most circulated cartoon among college newspapers for 5 years running. After that I had a development contract with King Features which didn't pan out. Then, I wrote a comic with illustrator Orrin Brewster for Creators. It was called Color Blind and was the first cartoon, ever, to depict inter-racial parents. After 2 years Orrin quit the strip so we decided to end it.

WHEN REINDEER DREAM

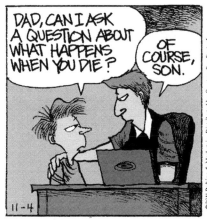

"Who gets your car," (top). Readers and newspaper editors sometimes accuse us of portraying a family that is too negative. I suspect that these individuals would rather we be "warm and fuzzy" — maybe add a little dog character, with big eyes. Heck, we'd probably be in more newspapers if we did. But we don't and we won't. Because that's not where the "funny" is. It's in real life, when a child, not yet armed with social graces, asks a question like that. Elliot's not a bad kid, or even a negative kid. He's just a kid who we're allowing to be a kid.

FROM THE "DADDY DICTIONARY"

Microwave

1. Pain-induced, minuscule, birdlike, flutter of the hand after opening the plastic on a microwave dinner before letting it sit for the recommended "one minute" (usually accompanied by a, "small scream, not unlike what one might hear from an nine-year-old girl"

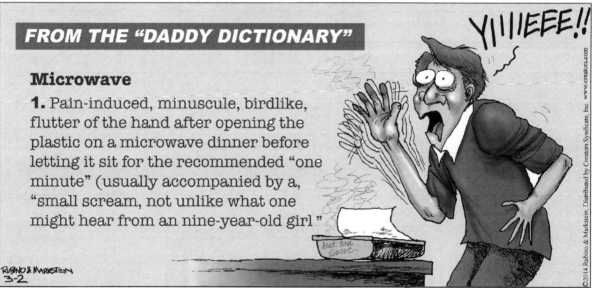

Gary's first national syndication gig was with Copley News Service in 1985. Not long after, he landed his first job as editorial cartoonist for the Mesa Tribune in Arizona — all steps on his path to award-winning work as political cartoonist for the Milwaukee Journal Sentinel.

I'm also an author, advertising art director and fine artist (and I use all those terms loosely). See my portfolios and links to my other ventures here: http://www.rubinocreative.com

Our characters are often aware that they are in a comic strip. We "break the fourth wall," as they say (top). In this case we shattered it.

Peg's nephew, Spork (center), is a new addition. He's a recent college graduate, staying with the gang while he tries to find employment. So far he's not trying very hard. It was Gary's idea to add the Spork character in order to bridge the generational gap between Elliot and his dad.

You might think that, as the writer, I get off easy when creating a comic with no dialog (bottom and page 129, center). Just the opposite. These are some of the most challenging cartoons to write and for Gary to illustrate.

Though we've been collaborating for nearly a decade, Gary and I have never met face to face. I know. Right?!

It's true, though. I live in New York City. Gary lives in Wisconsin. We never see each other and hardly ever speak — preferring to communicate via email — In fact, I'm not entirely certain that Gary actually exists. He may be an alter-ego I made up. You know, like Ed Norton did in that movie "Fight Club." Only, without the fighting... or the club... or Brad Pitt... or Edward Norton. Plus, he does exist... so it's not like that at all.

About Tony Rubino

Anthony Rubino, Jr., was born in New Jersey, a first-generation, Italian-American, Roman Catholic. Needless to say he developed a sense of humor at an early age … and then felt guilty about it. Combining, art, humor and the inability to do anything else, he found his calling in the careful study of drivel.

Tony is the co-creator of the internationally syndicated comic strip, *Daddy's Home*. His other cartoon syndication credits include national distribution by King Features and Tribune Media Services.

His latest book, Why Didn't I Think of That? Mediocre Inventions That Changed The World, is also an internationally syndicated, weekly column. Never a stickler for math, Tony wrote, Life Lessons from Your Dog as the fifth installment of his Life-Lessons book trilogy, which includes Life Lessons from Your Cat, Life Lessons from Elvis, Life Lessons from the Bradys, and Life Lessons from Melrose Place. Before that he displayed his steely work ethic by penning, 1001 Reasons to Procrastinate. And his fear of discomfort of eternal damnation is reflected in, Get Into Heaven Deck: Or Your Money Back. Along the way Tony has contributed his articles and cartoons to publications such as: MAD Magazine, Cracked, National Lampoon, the Chicago Tribune, and The Washington Post.

Tony's designs, comics and words can also be found on greeting cards and other product lines such as calendars, posters, and apparel sold in stores and catalogs worldwide.

His paintings and prints have been featured in galleries in New York, Chicago, Washington, DC and Los Angeles.

When not working on his writing and art in New York City he spends his time not working on his writing and art in New York City.

http://www.rubinocreative.com/

RUBINO & MARKSTEIN www.creators.com   ©2009 Rubino & Markstein. Distributed by Creators Syndicate, Inc.

About Gary Markstein

Award-winning editorial cartoonist and "Daddy's Home" illustrator, Gary Markstein began his cartooning career while doodling in the margins of his grade-school homework. One of his first caricatures was of Richard Nixon, drawn in a fifth-grade drafting class. "My classmates went crazy over it, and I was hooked," he says.

Markstein majored in graphic design at Arizona State University, where he drew a popular comic strip for the college newspaper. In his editorial freelance work no political figure was safe from his cutting- edge commentary. This resulted in national syndication with Copley News Service in 1985. Not long after, he landed his first job as editorial cartoonist for the Mesa Tribune in Arizona — all steps on his path to award-winning work as political cartoonist for the Milwaukee Journal Sentinel.

His numerous cartooning awards include the John Fischetti Award in 1997; 2001 and 2002 Global Media Awards; and the Ranan Lurie/United Nations Cartoon Award in 2004.

Markstein's work has been featured in many publications, including Newsweek, Time and U.S. News and World Report.

Today, as co-creator of Daddy's Home, Markstein says many of the antics in the strip are reflected in his home life with his two sons. However, he contends he is an excellent cook, contrary to what his sons might say.

https://garymarkstein.carbonmade.com
http://www.gocomics.com/garymarkstein

Other *Daddy's Home* Links

Read The Latest *Daddy's Homes*, or Have It Sent Directly to Your Mail Box Every Day:
http://www.gocomics.com/daddyshome **or** *http://www.creators.com/comics/daddys-home.html*
Visit The *Daddy's Home* Store: *http://www.cafepress.com/daddyshomestore*
Like *Daddy's Home* on Facebook: *on.fb.me/1is667K*
Follow *Daddy's Home* on Twitter: *https://twitter.com/daddyshomepete*

Other Stuff By Tony Rubino

Other Books By Tony Rubino: *http://www.amazon.com/Anthony-Rubino/e/B001JRVHJQ/ref=ntt_dp_epwbk_0*
Why Didn't I Think Of That? 101 Inventions That Changed The World By Hardly Trying, (Adams Media)
Life Lessons from Elvis, (Thomas Nelson)
Life Lessons from Your Dog (Thomas Nelson)
Life Lessons from Your Cat, (Thomas Nelson)
Life Lessons from the Bradys, (Plume)
Life Lessons from Melrose Place (Adams Media)
1001 Reasons to Procrastinate (CCC)
The Get Into Heaven Deck: Or Your Money Back (Collectors Press)

Tony Rubino (Main Website): *http://www.rubinocreative.com*
Rubino Fine Art: *http://tony-rubino.artistwebsites.com*
Rubino Fine Art on Etsy: *https://www.etsy.com/shop/RubinoFineArt*
Custom Portraits and Fine Art By Tony Rubino: "The Art of You":
https://www.etsy.com/shop/RubinoArtOfYou?ref=ss_profile
Like Rubino Fine Art on Facebook: *on.fb.me/1jbSRH8*
Follow Rubino Fine Art on Twitter: *https://twitter.com/RubinoCreative*

Other Stuff By Gary Markstein

Gary Markstein Website: *https://garymarkstein.carbonmade.com*
Editorial Cartoons By Gary Markstein: *http://www.gocomics.com/garymarkstein*

Made in the USA
Middletown, DE
20 November 2017